My Diamond in the Desert

By Concepción Carolina Vásquez

Printed in the United States of America

KMP Entertainment (Publishing Division)
www.kmpentertainment.org

DIAMOND IN THE DESERT

Our city embraces the multi-cultural diversity of our community
Our Franklin Mountain with the Star
The city divided by the Rio Grande
To the north the red, white and blue colors of the American Flag
and
To the south the red, white and green colors of the Mexican Flag
Each facet has a different color of the desert and represents the
many people that make our diamond brilliant

DEDICATION

I write these memories because I want to highlight the life of three great women that forged the human being that I am today.

My mother Delia Lara Carbajal. She was the only daughter of a marriage that was legendary for their love and she was conceived after a lengthy period that proved the devotion that her parents Carolina and Roberto had for one another and the respect for their traditions and values. My grandfather was a 7th generation Texan reared in an area that was mainly Hispanic but where people loved being American and had tremendous respect and love for the US. Her mother's parents were also from the border area but with deep Hispanic roots that came to this country because their government was totally against people that were self sufficient and tried to destroy them for being successful so they chose to move to the US and pledge their allegiance to the new country. Never looked back.

My grandmother, Carolina Carbajal, was an example of a faithful beautiful wife that lived for her husband and her daughter, my mom Delia. She was truly the perfect housewife and mother.

My great Aunt Josefina Carbajal de Chavez. Was the eldest daughter of Jose Maria Carbajal and Concepcion Escajeda de Carbajal both from families that came to the new world from Europe. This great aunt took care of my mom when her mother died, since mom was only 6 years old. Later on in life, the same aunt took care of me while my mom was busy working to support me. During that period, both mom and I, lived in Baja California. Mom emigrated into Mexico becoming a powerful, well-known woman that excelled in her chosen work. She later returned to the US until her death in 2024 when she was 93 years old.

PREFACE

There is a little sliver of Texas in the great Lone Star State that is unique. It is called: La Isla (The Island). Some of my ancestors are from this area. Their spirit and uniqueness have impacted me throughout my life. My paternal grandfather, Jesus Vasquez Sr, settled there. With his kin they built homes mainly from Adobe which to date stand in this arid part of Texas. It is an agricultural area.

His wife, Ramona Cano (Lujan) Vasquez was the last wife of my grandfather. She was mother of nine children and step mother to the many children my grandfather had with various women and wives prior to marrying her. Ita Mona (Abuelita Ramona) was the illegitimate daughter of Leonardo Lujan whose family lived in San Elizario and whose grandparent was one of the founders of the first County Board in the Area.

My grandfather also was the first person asked to be responsible for the distribution of water for the agricultural area in the Lower Valley. This family left the area after the Salt Wars with the Anglos and fights with the US Cavalry. They dispersed all over and sold their land in San Elizario. Only my grandmother remained in the area as she had married a man that was a rancher and pistolero.

The Lujan family thought she was never recognized by her father, but they loved her and would always visit her in her ranch. To my grandmother, it did not matter who the wives were, just that you were of the same blood, you were kin and you were loved regardless of how you were conceived. She always welcomed her husband's children and told them the ranch was theirs because it belonged to their father. She promoted unity and love amongst the family. She said "I am the last wife, that is what matters."

What was so unique in La Isla? After a hard rain, they would either wake up on the Mexican side or on the American side. The question of the day was: Good morning, what are we today Mexican or American? It really did not matter as, culturally to date, we are mostly of Hispanic Ancestry. But our national and political entity will always be American. We were never taught to feel different from the Anglos in the area, as we mingled and befriended everyone. We all spoke both languages.

The neighboring communities did not share this event, but the dual identities is something that is either a positive or a negative trait, depending on how you want to view your status. My family always viewed our status as a positive. We were the children of the Southwest, a merging of mainly three cultures the natives, the immigrants from Mexico, Spain or the Anglo world, but united under one flag and one nation of our beloved USA.

We were all reared to believe that we are special, recipients of great cultures and had the ability to choose the best from each but always respecting what we decided to leave behind...because we are the product of the past.

My elders always insisted that we learn, respect and appreciate our roots. They taught us to love and participate in the continuous building of this great nation, the USA.

So this is the story of my family, the Vasquez-Lujan Cano family, from my father, and the Lara Dutchover-Carbajal Escajeda who were my mom's parents. It's equally the story of Fabens and San Elizario, Texas from the county of El Paso. I call this area the Diamond in the Desert.

My artist friend Stephanie Conroy heard me talking about this area when she had her studio in San Elizario. This little town was moving from a historical area to one that embraced art at that time. Various artists started opening their studios in this historical town. Combining History and Art gave it an alluring magic and she gave a painting depicting the area as a "Diamond in the Desert" because of my love for this extremely beautiful part of West Texas.

CHAPTER ONE

"Roots of the families"

My ancestors were in this area since it was part of Spain, Mexico, the Republic of Texas and USA. When the Mexican revolution made it impossible for one of my ancestors to care for their families in Mexico, they returned to the USA in 1912. They settled in the border town of Fabens, Texas. They opened a store called "Las Dos Banderas" or in English "The Two Flags."

I think this title accurately describes me as well. I behave as a living product of the Hispanic culture but being born in the USA. I am an American with no other national allegiance than to the United States of America. The family had lived in the Southwest years before Texas attained its independence from Mexico and became a Republic and prior to the Treaty of Guadalupe Hidalgo in 1850 when the border was defined between Mexico and the USA.

Being descendants of the first Spanish colonizers, their language was Spanish. There was no loyalty to Mexico as a country since it was just forming, but to the Spanish culture instead. Definitely, there was a connection to the culture since they were all a blend of Native and European in various degrees.

My mother's family left the United States because the laws and the language began to change. They found it difficult to function in a Protestant English speaking country when they were Catholic and Spanish speakers. The treaty of Guadalupe

Hidalgo was supposed to protect Hispanics from loosing their heritage, their language and their lands. Instead, they found themselves feeling ostracized in the land that they called home for hundreds of years so they left and crossed the border to the nascent Republic of Mexico. Mexico was also going through its challenges as the now native-born Mexicans from Spanish and Indian families were also struggling to break the ties with Europe and get rid of a Monarchy imposed by Napoleon III.

Mexican President Benito Juarez and USA President Abraham Lincoln had forged a friendship which stalled the aggressive quest for land of the USA. But soon after President Lincoln was assassinated, the USA invaded Mexico. The Americans took half of Mexico's territory and, for a small amount of money, forced Mexico to sell its land. To us, Hispanics, it was an unwarranted act of aggression, and one whose scars continue to be an open wound in our collective psyche.

CHAPTER TWO

"Two families as different as night and day"

My Mom's family and my Dad's family were quite different. The Carbajal's were merchants and strong believers in tradition, like their Spanish and Mexican roots. The Vasquez family was an agricultural family, protectors and nurturers of the land. I grew up with one family and did not interact with the other one until I became an adult. However, the blood was stronger than any interaction. I grew up adoring the land, loving the smell of flowers and fruits and instinctively tending gardens. I always rejoiced in seeing the growth of plants and enjoyed the fruits of the land, especially if I had any part of their growth.

Later in life, one of my uncles told me: You are a true Vasquez, tending the land is in your blood. Why are you surprised that you always have an herb and vegetable garden? It is in your genes! I was so proud to have the love of agriculture as part of my DNA. It was a blessing that came to me without effort, seemingly because I was the granddaughter of a farmer.

My parents were divorced before I was born. My mom got rid of anything related to my father and even tried to take my last name away. I have no idea why their marriage turned so sour, but it did, and I was caught in the middle of a very strong willed mother and a feeble spirited father. They both loved me, but in diverse ways.

Mother felt betrayed, and because of the Carbajal's intense sense of self and individuality, took upon her motherhood with tremendous pride and resolve. She could have been one of those mothers that believes in the choice of abortion, yet that never ever entered her mind. She only thought of how to bring up her child, and then set out to provide me with a life full of beauty, culture and possibilities that, to date. has been nurturing to my soul. She once told me "If I had to sweep the floor with my tongue, I would have, if that meant that I could provide without the help of your father."

I can surely understand how this attitude kept her afloat, but I was sorry that Father was not asked to participate in my education or to contribute to my wellbeing. She could have put this money in an account and given it to me when I became and adult. Instead, I got nothing from my father. He never even thought of me in his will.   So I got my secondary education by holding several jobs. It was difficult, but it helped me learn to support myself. I do not come from a family that asks for Government support, so I have always worked my way out of any financial hardship.

Misguided by pride, Mom wanted to take my last name and eradicate any vestige of the Vasquez in me, but I also was blessed to have an equally strong-willed paternal grandmother. Ita Mona was infuriated by this and fought Mother legally so that if my mother rejected her son, that was Ok, but the name was not negotiable. I was not a bastard child and even though my mother had full control of my life, she did not have the right to strip me of my last name.

This little event separated these two families, but it accomplished what my grandmother wanted. That was that I would always be a Vasquez, no matter if I did not have contact with her family at all. I never knew this story until I met my grandmother the day I was married, and I finally heard the other side of my life story. I was forever grateful to this woman and grew to be close to her until her death.

Life took mother and I to another state and another country. Even though both my parents and their families were from the US, I ended up growing up in Mexico, in the border of Mexicali/Calexico in California.

I had a unique experience, as mother was legally a US Immigrant working in Mexico. Since I was a minor, they did not even consider legalizing my status, so I ended up living close to 18 years as an undocumented US citizen. I did not like this feeling as I was always afraid that my status would be known.

I surely can sympathize with the children that live here in this country without papers. You are an innocent victim of ignorance or circumstance, but you have no say so and your only option is to cope and hide. In Mexico is it extremely difficult, since you cannot move from one area to another without parental approval, and I saw firsthand the power of money as I moved around with bribes from my maternal great aunt who was, by all intents and purposes. the most influential person in my life. She always protected me.

My aunt was the oldest sister of my maternal grandmother who died when my mom was only 6 years old. She had come to Mexico with her husband from Fabens, Texas. They lived with lots of needs while my Mom was growing up but had managed to come upon an emerging industry and my great uncle started three radio stations in Baja California. So all their hard work was crowned with tremendous financial and social success.

My Mom brought me to Mexico to an extremely affluent lifestyle. I grew up with a cook, a personal maid, a gardener and a security guard. I frankly thought that everyone had this same lifestyle. I had no idea that I was part of the elite in my city. I think it helped that my great aunt had grown up in the US where rank and money are not factors in evaluating a person.

Thanks to this one US value, the servants were treated like equals and as members of our family. I was shocked when I learned how people that I had in high esteem had very strange behaviors when dealing with the service. I have never liked this very odious part of Latin American society. The class issue is something that is totally alien for most Americans and completely abhorrent.

I remember this very elegant and successful woman (My great aunt) asking the maids to forgive her for not eating with us when company arrived, or apologizing for her arrogant friends when they acted in a despicable manner. I felt so proud of her and consequently have never felt that money or rank are the definite values of a person but the integrity and humanity of an individual which make them privy to respect.

This lady was the founding rock of my personality. She taught me about hard work, responsibility, respect and the need to know about history, roots, family values, the arts, travel, world cuisine, crafts, gardening as well as how to wash, clean, iron, sew, sweep, mop, cook and be a leader. She always told me: If you are to teach anyone anything or guide someone, you need to know how to do what you are asking others to do. I have never forgotten that I must first learn how to master anything before I can ask someone to do it for me.

Living in the lobby to hell as the Imperial Valley is known (La ante Sala del Infierno), she and I traveled to Texas and Mexico every year. We visited family for a whole month or two, and I was her constant companion visiting all her innumerable kin in Texas. The month of September we always spent it in Mexico City with her daughter. We traveled around Mexico and she would always demand that our first event upon arriving was to visit our blessed mother of Guadalupe. In Mexico you are first a Guadalupana and then a Catholic. It is not necessary to be a Catholic to be a Guadalupana. Some people forget that the Southwest was part of the Spanish Colonies when Our Blessed Mother of Guadalupe appeared therefore she is the mother of even us in this land of the US without us being part of Mexico.

CHAPTER THREE

"The trek from Guadalupe, Distrito Bravo, Chihuahua - Mexico to Fabens, Texas – USA"

Some years ago, our family was gathered by a Professor of the University of New Mexico who had found a book about our ancestors: "La Familia Carbajal." The book was written by an author whose last name was Toro. She had traced us and asked us to gather in the Town of Las Cruces, New Mexico to introduce us to her scholarly project of translating this book into English and inform us about the family that she believed we were a part of.

We were curious, so some of us went to see what this project was all about. During this meeting we discovered that our family had Jewish roots.

Wow, what a revelation! Most of us, are staunch Catholics and having Jewish ancestry was a surprise to say the least. But some things began to make sense. Like my great grandfather's relationship with a leading Jewish person in El Paso who befriended him since he lived in Mexico and was his supplier for years when he trekked annually to El Paso to supply his store in the town of Guadalupe.

My great grandfather had been the mayor of this town and he was a businessman. He had a strong sense of family, responsibility, work ethic and strong ties to his Spanish ancestry. His parents were Spanish and when his daughters were married, he had mantillas brought from Spain for their marriage.

For years, in the family house in Fabens, there was an impressive painting of President Porfirio Diaz that had been given by the Mexican President to our great grandfather: Jose Maria Carbajal. They were friends and due to this "Papa Ia" as we called him, was not too thrilled with the Mexican Revolution since it was against his friend Don Porfirio. I will not even attempt to evaluate this relationship or attempt to align myself with what was right or wrong on this issue but in my house, the great President Benito Juarez was known as Beno and Pancho Villa was no more than a bandit and a savage not the folk hero venerated by our young Hispanics nowadays.

Years ago a famous painter and historian of the southwest Jose Cisneros gave me a beautiful print that he had illumined of Don Luis De Carbajal an illustrious governor of San Luis Potosi during the time of the Inquisition. I do not know if it is conclusive that we are descendants of this particular branch of this famous Carbajal family.

Most of them died during the Mexican Inquisition when it was discovered that they had Jewish ancestry. Don Luis de Carbajal who was the

Governor of one Spanish area was burned alive as were most of his family and relatives. Those that survived may have been the ones that settled in San Elizario and Fabens or they may have come to the SW with the famous Onate expedition. None the less, the Carbajal family had Jewish roots and came from Spain.

Years ago there was a play in Mexico City called: "La familia Carbajal", the Carbajal family and it depicted this family's travails and demise in the Spanish Empire now Mexico. Some of my cousins went to see it and they tell me, it was enlightening and sad.

Whether we are, or not, is irrelevant. What matters is that we discovered our roots and now we know that our family is part of what we call Crypto

Jews. Jews that left Europe during the Inquisition and embraced Christianity to survive. Many just pretended to be Christians, carefully guarding their Jewish traditions. Many did change religions, though. As time went by, I don't know whether they just forgot their roots or were really converts. They were called "Marrano" families. Calling someone a pig family is not very alluring. This I am certain came about because Christians eat pork which is forbidden and if you are Jewish, they were then considered traitors by their own people.

I ended up going to Israel soon after this meeting since I wanted to know what being Jewish is all about. I did visit Israel and mingled with Jews, Arab Christians, Druze and Bedouins but not with

Muslim Israelis. I went a third time exclusively to visit the WALL and had the most fascinating experience.

I was taken to the Wall by a Jewish Israeli who had never been to the Christian sites, so he visited these areas with a Catholic and I visited the Israeli Chirstian areas with a Jew. We both learned how to respect each other views and continue being friends plus I had a wonderful encounter with the God of Israel.

When I touched the wall, I felt a bolt of lighting hitting me and was embraced by a feeling of love and protection. It caused me to start crying and whaling. Now I know why it is called the whaling wall. I could not stop crying until I felt all my moral pain go away. I was a mess and totally disheveled joined by Jewish friend who told me. Connie you a

Catholic from US have an encounter with my God and I that was born here have never experienced his presence. I told him that it was probably because Jesus was a Jew and his God is the Jewish God, the one Jews worship. This experience has given me the directive to always defend the rights of the Jewish People and respect the Jewish God as my own. Jesus Father Abba.

Through the years I visited Israel Again in Christmas 2022. I went to the Holy Land to celebrate Christmas. I had wanted to do this all my life. At this point, Mom had developed full- blown Dementia. I was taking care of her in order to help her cope with this horrible decease. I was falling apart and needed some moral guidance, so I decided to go to Bethlehem. It was a fabulous trip that I took by myself, visiting both Jewish and Muslim friends living in Israel and Palestine.

I celebrated Mass on Holy night in Bethlehem, and Hannukah in Tel Aviv with my Jewish friends. It was memorable.

Something fabulous happened on Holy night. My Palestinian Muslim Friend got me a ticket to attend the mass, and I was there during the day visiting the place where Jesus was born. There was a huge line and people in front that had been in line for over three hours. I prayed for divine intercession. I got this brilliant idea of going to the front of the line and asked their indulgence in permitting me to enter because I was a senior citizen that had travelled the whole day from America and was exhausted. I would not be able to stand in line for many hours in order to enter. With the help of God, they let me in and escorted and helped me enter the cave and get on my knees to touch the star where Baby Jesus was placed after his birth. I was beyond joyous for the opportunity granted me.

I was able to hear mass, have holy communion with hundreds of Catholics from all over the world and the Patriarch of Bethlehem gave me permission to kiss baby Jesus that he had in his arms, on his way to place him on the star that I had visited earlier. On my way out of the church the procession stopped by where I was standing and I ended up face to face with the Patriarch and, of course, I asked if I could pay my respects to Baby Jesus. I guess my gray hair made this possible. Sometimes being of age has its advantages!!

So this trip confirmed that I had Jewish blood and I was elated and grateful. Even if I have one drop of Jewish blood, I feel blessed.

I don't know if Papa Ia, my great grandfather knew about his Jewish roots or not, because this was never discussed. His wife, Mama Concha, was very Catholic and passed on her faith to all my great aunts including my grandmother. One of our strongest family traditions is our reverence to the Blessed Sacrament. I have my great-grand-mother's prayer devotional, and it seems she used to make it a practice to spend time with the Blessed Sacrament. This is an activity that to date is one of the favorite practices of my faith. I used to engage in this activity with another of my great aunts, the last one to pass away not too long ago. Any time we had a problem, we were taught to go visit the Blessed Sacrament and talk over our problems with our blessed Jesus. I am not much into Saints or formal prayers but definitely into always having a personal dialogue with the Holy Trinity basically though the Holy Sacrament. I have spent numerous times in any church by the Blessed Sacrament discussing my travails and tribulations and asking for guidance.

So what did this family of staunch Catholics do with this newly acquired fact that we are descendants of Jews? One of my eldest cousins went to one of the local synagogues and registered herself in their roster in order to belong and explore more about her roots. The rest of us decided to celebrate these roots during one of our bi-annual Christmas

Celebrations. I guess it's not very Jewish to celebrate the birth of the Messiah they deny!!

Anyway, Christmas was coming up, so we all gathered different Jewish recipes and each one of us prepared one. Instead of having ham or turkey, we had lamb and an array of Jewish delicacies during our Christmas dinner. We bought CDs of Jewish music and managed to badly recreate some Jewish dances. We had so much fun. Unfortunately, it did not continue, it was a one occasion event. We really knew nothing about being Jewish and for most of the family it was too laborious to keep it up. So this one time Jewish celebration of our roots is now a distant memory.

In my case it was different. I had married a Muslim and had been brainwashed to believe that

Jews were the scum of the world. Having discovered my Jewish ancestry, I obviously had to re-evaluate this belief and thankfully I no longer hold this view. As a matter of fact, I became a defender of the Jewish People and now notice all the Jewish based practices that we have as Catholics. I have developed and nourished a love for the Holy Land and all its people, Jews, Muslims, Arabs, Druze, and Bedouins. Every opportunity I have, I will continue to visit and learn from this great land, Israel the birthplace of Jesus.

So, going back to my family… "Papa Ia" lived peacefully in Guadalupe, Distrito Bravo, Chihuahua until the "Villistas" took over the town and decided to use his priced grand piano as a meat cutting board. He was horrified after this encounter with the simple uncouth farmers of the revolution and promptly gathered his family, whatever positions they valued, cashed as much money as he could and placed his family in a wagon. Deciding to move north back to the land of his forefathers. He left his house, land, acquaintances and business in the spur of a moment. He concluded his family was in danger and so he did what responsible parents do: protect his family, even if that meant to leave everything he had acquired and loved, so be it.

He sent his wife and children on the border of El Paso but he entered the USA on a carriage back in 1911. But since he had relatives in the area, mainly San Elizario, he settled in the town of Fabens, which is now about less than 50 miles from El Paso and about 10 miles from San Elizario.

This is a picture of the Carbajal home taken in 2000. It still had three doors in the front with three windows and it was just an adobe square. I could never figure out why the home was a massive square with few windows and no formal distinguished living room, but after hearing how this structure came to be, it makes sense. My great aunts recounted that they arrived in winter. Back then winters in this area were not so mild. They were permitted to live in a school while he set out to build a house for them.

With whatever money he had, he hired as many workers as he could. Some say that up to 100 workers were hired, and the house was built in about three weeks. It was a massive adobe shell where he sheltered his family and started his new business. His Jewish friend, Mr. Schwartz of El Paso, having been a business associate for years, gave him credit and thus the first Carbajal store was born. It was called "Las Dos Banderas".

Up till 2010, one of his granddaughters had the Furniture store in Fabens. This store had many reincarnations, Las Dos Banderas, General Store and finally Carbajal Furniture. She held on to it for years even though she was in failing health and none of her children wanted to follow the tradition. Lovingly, she held to our family roots until she finally closed.

This is the warehouse. A sign there read serving the Valley

since 1911

I was very little when my great-grand-father passed away and the only memory I have of him is eating strawberry Jell-O. He loved Jell-O and during his later years, as he lay bedridden on a small hospital bed in the family home, I used to peak through a door looking at him eat his Jell-O. He was very white with completely gray hair. Remembering him now reminds me of an Apostle of the Old Testament. A loving elder, whose mere presence in the household gave the family comfort.

As a child I was terrified of him. I don't think they could ever get me to get close to him. But he used to see me from his bed and I would be there for hours looking at him. Little did I know what an influence this man would have for the rest of my life. I was his first great granddaughter. I am sure he was just as curious about me as I was about him but I don't think we ever crossed a word. At those times, children were taught to be invisible. We were seen but not heard. My great grandmother had died years before in Mexico when she went to visit her oldest granddaughter. She died in Veracruz, the place where the Spaniards first arrived in Mexico. I remember visiting her grave with my great aunts when they decided to bring her remains back to El Paso.

I had two great aunts that acted as surrogate grandmothers. They will always hold a very special place in my life. It is as if they are my guardian spirits throughout my life, giving me spiritual succor and comfort along my travails. They have been gone for many years, but their presence is still felt, to this day. My great grandfather settled in Fabens running his merchandise and general store and moved it various times within the same block. First, he separated it from his house once it was up and running, and then it was later moved because it burned to the ground.

My great grandfather reared his family in this little town, and gave his children as much education as he could. He sent his son to study in the town of San Elizario, which was the county seat for many years and not the sleepy town it is today. Later he was sent to El Paso to study accounting in order to continue his retail business.

The daughters were not given as much attention in those days. Women were meant to get married, so not much emphasis was given to their education. Nonetheless, all the Carbajal children were taught to read and write and given a love for books and reading. They may not have had a formal education, but they were not illiterate and they knew about art, history and geography. The one that took this learning more at heart was my great aunt Josefina, "Tia Fina." She was the one that, from a stroke of luck, ended up rearing me in Baja California. But I will tell you about her later on.

"Papa Ia" ended up being a respected and successful member of this town. The family recounts that he and Mr. Fabens tossed a coin to name the town. So it is possible that instead of the town now being known as Fabens, it could have been the City of Carbajal.

"Papa Ia" was also a man of strong opinions and beliefs. One Sunday someone stole his hat and he decided churchgoers were thieves and hypocrites so he stopped going to church. Despite his wife's pleas, he never again went inside any church.

CHAPTER FOUR

"A love story Texas style, enormous"

Every family has a love story and the story of my maternal grandparents has been my inspiration. My grandfather Roberto is the one who taught me to love Texas. He claimed he was a 7th generation Texan. When he died, a Texas legislator gave me a flag that had flown in the State Capitol in Austin so that I could place it inside his coffin. He loved Texas and passed along his love for this land to me.

One time I was in tears recounting to him what a person had told me. I am very opinionated, and I cannot even remember what brought about this man's reaction. I guess he could not fathom that a brown skinned, Hispanic girl could have an opinion and he bluntly blurted that I should just go back to where I came from. I was shocked, angry and startled to the point that I could not even speak. I went to my grandfather and blurted out my encounter with this very despicable, racist man.

My grandfather listened to me and, soothing my bruised ego, told me to calm down. He then proceeded to tell me about his family in East Texas and how I had nothing to be ashamed of. As a matter of fact, he told me, "your family was here before these racists even new this land existed." He told me "You never let them belittle you or question your right to be in this country. You are a proud Texan and you are where you belong"

He said that his family's encounter with an English-speaking person had caused a commotion in the sheep herding community where they lived, in what is now Fort Davis, Texas. This foreigner arrived speaking something that no one understood. They thought the man was crazy, so they put him in a corral and waited for him to calm down. Someone in the community figured out the man was not crazy, but was speaking a foreign tongue, which happened to be English. Back then, in this part of Texas, people only spoke Spanish not English. So there, my grandfather put my heritage into perspective. From that point on, I never let anyone question my right to call myself a Texan. The lesson here is that information, especially historical information gives one power to defend oneself against discrimination and ignorance.

My grand father's family was not only Spanish but from a Nordic country. His grandfather seems to have married an Comanche lady. He descends from a family called Dutchover and from the pictures I have seen, he was a tall, red head and his wife a short, brown eyed Native American. So love in my family has transcended race and religion since its beginning in this land of ours.

Back in those days, marriages were arranged and you just followed and accepted when your family decided to marry you. My grandfather Roberto was no exception. He, like his parents, was born in Fort Davis. He was born in 1904 but moved to Balmorhea in 1914. His family had arranged his marriage and he was to marry a lady from Las Cruces,

New Mexico so he dutifully got on a train to meet his future wife whom he had never seen.

Trains in those days, as well as train stations, were the life blood of towns. They brought supplies, commercial goods, food and of course new people into the community. Fabens is and was a small town even then. The arrival of the train was a main activity and grand occasion for the inhabitants of this town in West Texas.

My grandmother Carolina, her sisters and friends waited every time for the train in anticipation. They would get all decked up and go to the station to see the train, the goods it brought and the new people who arrived. On such a day, my grandfather, a young man from Balmorhea, Texas, happened to be on this train on his way to Las Cruces. The train stopped in

Fabens and my grandfather got out to get some refreshments and see the town while it was unloaded. As he got out, he noticed a group of young girls, and he saw my grandmother. He was smitten! She was young, beautiful and full of life and cheer. He fell in love with her. It was love at first sight. He gathered his belongings from the train and got out. He found a room to stay in, and proceeded to find out all he could about this young lady.

What an impact my grandmother must have made on him that gave him the courage to defy his family, abandon his future bride and seek out a completely different lifestyle. There were no sheep in Fabens at the time, so he had to leave all he knew and make a fresh start. He decided this in a split second. He had found the love of his life and he was not about to let this opportunity pass him by. How many of us have the courage to follow our heart? I know that up till now, I surely have not.

Years later, when my grandfather was in his upper nineties, my mom used to tease me that no matter what I did, my grandfather would always find an excuse for my behavior. I did no wrong in his eyes. Grandfather used to tell me that I was the only tie he had to the love of his life. When my grandmother died, he remarried and had a very successful and loving marriage, but not like the searing love that only happens once in any lifetime that he had with my grandmother.

Every year, I place a Christmas decoration of the "Hotel Del" in my Christmas tree to honor where I came from, and the love of my grandparents. Del

Coronado Hotel in San Diego, California is where my grandparents spent their honeymoon, and my mother was born exactly nine months to the day they were married. My mom was a true love child. My grandparents love lasted way beyond death and time.

My grandmother was a child when my grandfather met her, maybe 15years old. My great grandmother had a very special relationship with her. Of all her children, my grandmother was the favorite and they were very close. When my grandfather entered the picture, it was not an easy relationship. My great grandparents were now successful people, and they were not about to let their favorite child marry an unknown man, so grandfather had a tough time ahead of him.

The men of this era were tough beyond comparison. Especially my grandfather. He decided to prove his worth, not just in word but in deed. He waited for my grandmother until she was 21 years old, as my great grandparents decided that she was way to young and inexperienced to marry so young. He, in this period, managed to build a successful business. He had a pool hall and not until he had enough to satisfy his future in-laws' requirements in character and economically, was he allowed to marry their daughter, almost seven years later.

Can you imagine waiting so many years, having to prove yourself year after year? This was true love, as he never wavered. Not for one moment. It reminded me of Biblical Jacob waiting for Rachel year after year. And his love for Joseph and Benjamin was above the love of all his other children. The children of love are always special. Love is not planned, it just happens. When it is true, it moves mountains.

My love-stricken grandfather waited years to marry Carolina, his wife. And, by all accounts, it was a marriage made in heaven. They loved each other and they had fun. As I had mentioned before, my mom was born exactly nine months from the date of their marriage. So they consummated their marriage and had a little girl whom they adored, my mom Delia Guadalupe.

Grandmother was a beautiful woman. Many say she was the prettiest of all the Carbajal sisters. She was white as snow and had the darkest black hair. But more than that, she was classy and elegant. She loved wearing hats and the latest fashions. As soon as

Mom was born, she made sure they both had matching outfits. My grandfather also always wore a beautiful hat and suits.

Back in those days, social life was very active in the Lower Valley. From El Paso to Tornillo, Texas are a series of small towns and they constantly had dances and plays. These were beautiful affairs with orchestras, and all the young people participated in the theatrical endeavors. I have found dance cards and programs of some of their activities. This era is long gone, even when I was young, but my grandparents were one of the most popular couples in the area. The people from that era, at least in my family, spoke English but their roots were Hispanic and they celebrated their Hispanic Culture, specially in poems and cultural readings.

Mother was very big when she was born and my grandmother became frail after giving birth. They did not have any more children and she had to take care of herself. When mother was about 6 years old, her parents went to a party in the middle of winter and grandmother caught a cold which turned into pneumonia. Penicillin had not been discovered in 1936 so she got sicker and sicker until she passed away, leaving a very small child who had only ever known the bliss of having two loving parents and a very large family.

Within a week, the most important person in my Mom's life disappeared leaving her with her father, who was in so much pain, he forgot all about his daughter.

Grandfather started drinking and eventually lost all the economic stability he had worked so hard to attain. His daughter was taken care of by her grandmother, Mama Concha. But Mama Concha was old and soon after asked her oldest daughter Josefina to take care of her since she was the one who had a more stable marriage and was a true caregiver.

My grandparents had moved to a little apartment adjacent to Mama Concha's house. As a matter of fact, they connected. My grandmother never learned how to cook, except for the basics. Every day, she would serve her husband wonderful dishes prepared by her mother and serve them in her beautiful dining room. Like I had mentioned before, mother and daughter were inseparable and when my grandmother died, her mother, as well, went into mourning. She changed her dress to black. She always wore a Spanish black mantilla and every day from that point forward she mourned her favorite daughter. No activity ever again gave her the incentive to wear colored clothing. She was sad until she passed away herself.

This was not a healthy environment for my mother and she was taken away to California to live with her oldest living aunt. That is why she and I ended up living most of our lives away from Texas. We would come every year to Fabens, but our home was the border towns of Calexico, California and Mexicali, Baja California.

Grandfather's world came crashing down in a matter of weeks and he just wanted to disappear and die. Living next to his in-laws, they took care of him and his daughter. Eventually, my grandmother decided to find him a wife. You can imagine how much they loved him when they themselves wanted him to be happy again. They found him a wife from San Elizario and married him with the whole family's blessing. He just agreed, and the first years of his new married life were extremely turbulent.

His children did not know the caring loving father that lived with Mom those five years until much later. Grandfather learned to love his wife and all his children adored him until he passed away. He, in his later years, took care of his wife day and night. She suffered from Parkinson's disease and many times we could not understand anything she was saying, but we understood her loving, tender gaze and smile. Grandfather monitored her every move and was always grateful to her for all the love and care that she showered him with throughout their marriage. They ended up being married for over 50 years. They were always happy and loving amongst themselves, as well as to all the extended family. My mom ended up with five more siblings and they stopped having children when I was born. My youngest uncle is barely two years older than I am.

I grew up with my maternal grandparent's family and my grandfather was loved by everyone together with his wife and family. However, I never called this wonderful woman grandmother. I only called her by her first name Aurora, a fitting name since it means dawn. So I think of her as the sun that lightened my grandfather's life until she passed away.

No one can ever doubt that grandfather loved this lady and was a faithful loving husband but he always loved his first wife, all the days of his life.

One year, my Mom's curiosity allowed her to discover Grandfather's carefully guarded secret. Every year on a specific day, rain or shine grandfather would disappear from early in the morning until late at night. Mother followed him and discovered it was on the date of the anniversary of her mother's death. Grandfather would go to the cemetery and recount to my grandmother what his year had been like. For hours he would tell her all he did during that previous year and at times would just cry. On the ground would hug the cold stone that held her.

Imagine my mother's surprise and the shame she felt for following him and discovering his secret.

Not a word was ever said but now we all understood the character of this man and the immense love that he still had for his deceased wife, decades after her death. He did this until one year from his death at age 96 when he became so ill he could no longer go on his own.

Having proof that this type of love exists, I always wanted something similar for myself. Once I asked him: grandfather, do you love Aurora, your present wife? And, he said: "Yes, with all my heart, but your grandmother was and will always remain the love of my life. I hope you will find someone that loves you as much as I loved my wife." Well, that remains my hope to date. He gave me the ring that she wore when they got married and I always wear it when I am going through difficult times and need their spiritual support, it gives me comfort. This is not a Hollywood story. This is real life, a real true love, the Texan way, enormous!

CHAPTER FIVE

"What do Texans do in California?"

Home is where your heart is and for Mom and I, home has always been Texas. Both of us were born in El Paso, but after her mother died, Mom grew up in California. That is where she went to school and, to date, has lifelong friends. But, our family was from Texas and we had very unique ways of celebrating, eating and behaving which have governed out lives wherever we go. I was four years old when I left Texas but I grew up in Baja California on the Mexican side of the border.

Everyone talks nowadays about losing one's identity or debate on what is an American. However, American is not just a person that lives in this country but one that embraces its values and loves it despite its shortcomings. To me, compared with the rest of the world, are minimal.

I always laugh when I hear people talking about being an illegal alien, as if you are a criminal. I confess I was an illegal alien but not because I wanted to. When you are a child, you just live where your parents take you to live. You have no say so. I lived in Mexico as an undocumented immigrant for 17 years. When I became an adult, I had to come back to the USA permanently, since now I did have a choice as to where to live and I was no longer a minor.

Mother grew up in Calexico, California a very small town in the border of California - USA and Mexicali, Baja California on the Mexican side. This city is the capital of the State of Baja California. She briefly moved to Texas when she married my father but when I was 4 years old moved back to California but on the Mexican side, to Mexicali. This town is where I grew up and where I learned to love the USA because of my mothers love for her country and my great aunt who had to give up her citizenship when her husband's business took her to Mexico.

At that time, foreigners in Mexico could not own property or if they did, it was not a controlling percentage. My great aunt had to give up being a USA citizen and become a Mexican citizen. All her life she longed for her citizenship and made me promise that the first thing I would do when becoming of voting age, would be to register and participate in the civic life as a citizen with all its responsibilities.

I was her driver when I became of age to drive. Prior to that, I was her constant companion, going with her everywhere. I was like her personal doll and it was imperative that I was well behaved as she was very socially active. Fortunately for me, her granddaughter lived in Mexico City and would only come for holidays, so I had her all to myself. Grandmothers and surrogate grandmothers are the most amazing individuals as they are willing to give you all their attention and love.

Almost daily, she would lament giving up her citizenship. I remember that during election time, I would take her to the polls. She was an early riser. Sow we'd often be the first ones there. Invariably the ballot boxes would be full even when she was the first voter. She would be so upset and would ask them:

Have you no shame? Obviously, she was totally against the regime at the time and always voted for the opposition.

She would turn to me and tell me: "You are an American citizen. In your country, votes are respected. Please don't ever forget that voting is an activity that is not respected everywhere in the world, as in the USA. You see this in Mexico, they are corrupt and my vote is worthless. I hope one day it will be respected but I may not see it in my lifetime." Sadly, she did not witness the Mexican transformation. It took many years after her death, for Mexico to have valid elections. She would have been so happy to witness the change and it did not take a violent revolution either.

Stereotypes are proven invalid in my family. Our family moved to Mexico for a better life, not the other way around. Mom was divorced, taking care of me while working as a receptionist for a doctor. Moving to Baja, she became a Radio Station Manager and one of the most prominent women in the country because of her job. At 26, she would meet and negotiate with the broadcasters, entertainers and syndicate heads. She would struggle with her Spanish, but she made sure that I had a proper language instruction, and she always spoke to me in English.

Mom and I lived in Baja. By this time my grand uncle had made a small fortune by becoming the owner of the first radio stations in Northern Mexico. He built his wife a mansion in the outskirts of town, to her specifications and that is the home I lived in until the business was sold to a conglomerate from Mexico City in the 70's and we again moved to the USA when my great aunt passed away.

Yes, I was the lucky one of the Carbajal's that lived in a Mansion all her life and had servants at her beck and call. I never lacked anything, I always thought everyone lived liked I did. We had lavish parties, were invited to the best events and met many personalities of the music world that paraded through my house since I was a little girl. I grew up with wonderful music, meeting interesting people and traveling with my great aunt three months our of the year. Mother introduced me to the world of Theater, ballets, plays, museums, fantastic restaurants and fabulous interesting people. I was always allowed to participate in the conversations which it was rare for my age but I loved to learn.

Our home was located in a block all by itself and one of the radio stations was on its side. So Mom could keep an eye on the business as well as on me.

Being a member of the media is fun. I had the latest music straight from the recording studios, so my parties were always with the most modern music and I knew all the newest information of all the movie stars in vogue. I met hundreds of personalities and was always aware.

Many years after I left Mexico, My grandfather told me a story that I have kept quiet. Since most of the relatives of that era are now dead, I can finally spill the beans. Grandfather told me that I always thought that the money my great uncle had made was due to his business skills which is true but with a twist. It seems that he was involved in drug trafficking and at the time. He had pulled the biggest drug heist, making him a huge amount of money.

With that money, he started the radio station which was the second radio station opened in Mexico after XEW in Mexico City. Mom was fortunate to ended up being the first woman radio station manager in Mexico and the first one to employ women as broadcasters and the first one to have a mobile unit ready to radio broadcast he news as they were happening.

Mom was always on top of the newest developments and willing to be the person that started many innovative ways to run a radio Station. She Participated in national events with the cream of the crop in broadcasting plus she always had great ideas.

Mom belonged to the Soroptimist Club and she used to come up with events that were good for the whole community.

She found out that the children in Mexicali that were blind did not have proper schooling. This prompted her to find someone who eventually donated some land, and then made many events to get monies to start a school for the blind. For a year she worked on different events, and finally they built the school and continued fundraising in order to maintain the school and pay the professors.

Mexico has a lots of social events so she decided to start a contest to permit underprivileged girls to become queens for an annual ball. Many of these girls worked for different businesses, and they would compete to have their employees become the recipients of the crown of Rosa de Mexicali. The Rose of the city of Mexical. Mother had the idea because I had become Queen of my school by selling tickets for the maintenance of it. So she transferred that model from a school to a business where all the business participated and young ladies that normally did not have the financial means became queens for a day. The socialites were not happy, but Mother was elated.

Another project my uncle had was to celebrate Mother's Day with the poorest mothers of the community. My mother would collect donations for flower bouquets and different musicians that would serenade mothers living in the poorest communities. The would sing for them in a radio show and give them a bouquet and different gifts from the different sponsors.

From 6 o'clock in the morning until night, Mother was taking these caravans all over the city. However, at noon she took her entourage to the Jail to celebrate mothers who were incarcerated. For an hour, she would give them a corsage and would take music and different artists to entertain them. Mom always thought of the most disadvantaged persons to help.

She always did such good work. She was constantly being given awards and recognitions. They wanted her to run to be a National Senator, but Mom was a US citizen and she would have had to give up her US citizenship, which she would never do. The Mexicans never understood, but Mom was an American. We always celebrated all the American holidays. Like Easter egg hunting, Memorial Day, Halloween, Thanksgiving. We were an American home in Mexico.

A funny thing happened. When living in Mexico I was the GRINGA. Never a Mexican and when I came to the US, I became the Mexican. Weird because I have never accepted any of these appellatives. I hate to be told what I am supposed to be. It is like being put in a cage.

I also had access to all the sporting events and my friends and I were always on the first rows of the most coveted games. I was very popular, but everything comes with baggage. Even then, the danger of being kidnapped was on my family's radar. We always lived cloistered with an armed guard in our home. No one could come to my home unless they were invited or notified us with plenty of time, so I missed out on having serenades like the rest of my girlfriends.

In Mexico, it is an extremely popular practice to take a serenade or live music to your girlfriend to declare your love. I missed this, as no one was allowed on the premises, and these things are done in the spur of a moment.

I thought that all the children that I knew had the same practices as I did, but afterwards I realized that this was not the case. I was very blessed to have a mother that made sure that I had the American experience, and she celebrated all the traditional holidays, though, as I said earlier.

For example: Halloween in October. Now it is celebrated all over the world, but when I was growing up the children on the Mexican side used to dress up and cross the border to Trick or Treat. For months we prepared our costumes, and Mother used to take me and my friends to the American side.

We admired the USA so much. Giving candy to total strangers was such a generous jest. We thought Americans were super. It was so much fun... until one dark day we encountered one of those racist people who started asking us a million questions and refused to give us candies because we were from Mexico. I can never explain what this does to a child. We were devastated and from that point on we were afraid to trick or treat. Our admiration turned to fear so we started having a big party at home instead and forwent the trips to the USA on this occasion.

Because of this experience, I have made it a point now living on the US side, to always have enough candy to treat all children, and I never ask them if they are American or not. It does not matter, in my book. Children should be nourished and this beautiful practice can be a unifier and not a divider. To deny a child a handful of candy seems to be a horrible way to act.

Easter egg hunting was another American custom we followed. Oh, what fun to be with your friends and look for candy in the form of eggs all over your garden! Though I was not a very good sport on this because I was so blind as a child. I could never see the darn eggs and everyone used to get them except me. All this came to an end when, one year, I was so frustrated I started crying and telling everyone to go home. So Mother had to send every child home. From that point on Mother always bought me a basket. She did this until I was way in my twenties, but the Easter egg hunts were suspended.

Valentine's day, is another American holiday that has reached the world. As a child, one made Valentines to all your friends, teachers and loved ones. It is somehow not the same as Friendship Day. That is like a watered down holiday trying to be more inclusive. We thought Americans were such loving people.

Ah! And those wonderful cook outs for Memorial, Labor and Independence Days. What a feast to have grilled hamburgers and hot dogs for one whole day. They would invite all their friends from the USA and we would have American music and they would talk about their high school days and life in the USA. I loved this mythical country that I was born in but did not know it until many years later.

And the mother of all holidays: Thanksgiving. Very few countries have a day to thank the Lord for all their blessings. Maybe because few are as blessed as we are? I'm thankful we have this unique day of prayer and gratitude. Every year as a child, we had a huge Turkey with all the trimmings and the adults would invite their closest friends. We would have a formal dinner, thanking God for all our blessings. I did not know that we were unique because I never discussed this holiday with my school friends. I just assumed everyone had it. But we were unique. We were Americans, in a foreign land, hanging on to our heritage and customs.

This holiday has taken bigger scale proportions for us here in the Southwest. We claim in El Paso to be the area when the American Southwest was born, and it all started with a thanksgiving years before the Pilgrims arrived in Massachusetts. I will explain later.

Every area has their special foods, and in our home we cooked Chihuahua or Tex Mex style. It is a very different cuisine from Mexican, Baja Californian or Californian food. For example cow tripe, red chili soup known as Menudo is unique to Chihuahua. You develop these food favorites and they last you a lifetime. Menudo is a favorite in my house after a party, early in the morning or late at night. It is a picker me upper and a delicious treat.

Enchiladas are a rolled corn tortilla stuffed with meat, onion and cheese; bathed with chili sauce and sometimes baked. In Texas, however, the tortillas are fried in oil and placed in a plate staking them with a layer of tortilla first, chopped onions and American cheese bathed in a chili sauce and then the process is repeated. They are quite delicious and filling, and all without meat. Nowhere else do they prepare them like in northern Chihuahua or Southwest Texas.

Another delicacy of El Paso is "Sopapillas." The city of San Elizario, Texas is supposed to be the birth place of this tasty treat. It is a white-flour bread fried in oil that rises up forming a little pocket. It is most delicious with fried eggs in the morning or peppered with cinnamon like a beignet and bathed with honey as a desert. Most of the typical Tex-Mex restaurants serve this in their menus.

Having lived on the Mexican side of the border has made me understand the dual life that we live. We are like chameleons. We enjoy and respect both cultures. Engaging in one holiday does not make us enemies but recipients of a dual enriching bilingual, bicultural life. Many of us can navigate into both cultures easily. However, many of us cannot. I think that is because we, as a people, have not learned both languages and do not know in depth both cultures. That is when we lose our identity and we do not know where to turn and our allegiances become blurred. Unfortunately, a number of people resist learning a second language. It makes me wonder: If they do not know where they came from how on earth can they ever expect to know where they are going?

CHAPTER SIX

"There are many Thanksgivings"

As Hispanics I think many times we feel like outcasts in our own land. Our heroes, our sacrifices, our history many times goes unnoticed. Nationwide all we hear about are the abuses, and the miseries. Rarely do we even know about our accomplishments and our contributions.

My father rarely spoke about his service during WWII. He and many of my uncles and relatives served in this war as Americans defending their country. That is why it is so painful when someone doubts our commitment and our love for this country.

I am not saying that many do not admire, love or respect the USA. Most of us do. It is our country, too. We want it to succeed and flourish like any other American.

I guess it is hard to understand that we have two flags. One is cultural, and the other one is our political and national identity. We are Americans first. Our commitment to this country is exemplified by how many of our Hispanic children are in the Armed Forces.

Probably the Armed Forces culture has changed, though. Many of the abuses our parents complained about are no longer there. However, in WWII, Mexicans and Blacks were always sent first in combat areas. They did not like it, but that is the way it was and they served with tremendous dignity and valor.

One such man was Guy Gabaldon who single-handedly, because of his look and his knowledge of Japanese, convinced the enemy to surrender to the tune of more than 1000 combatants. Do we hear about him? Of course not, very few people know about the heroism of this one Hispanic.

And the list goes on. We hear about Lafayette from France and his contributions to the American Revolution. Rarely, though, have I heard the story of Jose Galvez, a past Governor of Louisiana during the time it belonged to the Spanish Empire. He fell in love with the mission of our founding fathers and full of admiration for this new experiment in Democracy convinced the rich and powerful as well as just normal citizens of the Spanish colonies, now Mexico, to donate money to the American Revolution.

Millions of dollars in bullion were collected. He sent this treasure to General George Washington. This did not come from one government to another, but from one colonized people to another. Our founding fathers were not Hispanic, of course. But our ancestors did participate and helped in the colonies battle for independence. Was there a memorial or a monument anywhere in our nation's capital? No, not until very recently.

I know that recognition is hard to attain when you are a minority people but it has to come and many of us are working to this effect with varied degrees of success.

Amongst some very interesting contributions by Hispanics are some elementary icons of the American Southwest. What would you say they are?

What about the horse, the famous Mustang, that to date, roams the land in various parts of the US? This sturdy horse, the Mesteño, was brought by the Spaniards and introduced to the Southwest in various areas, but mainly through the Camino Real Trading Route which ends in Santa Fe, New Mexico and starts in Mexico City. This route passes through San Elizario and El Paso. Horses are not native of the USA. They were introduced to the Americas by the Spaniards, our ancestors.

What about the guitar, the main instrument used by the Country and Western musicians? This is an instrument descended of one used by the Moors of North Africa and evolving to what we call a modern guitar. As the Spanish explorers and conquistadors roamed the country stories of their feats became musical "corridos", this genre is alive in well with the ballads of the country and western genre.

Theater also started in this area. When the members of a Spanish Caravan arrived in the Rio Grande, (Rio Bravo to Mexicans), they recounted their trek by putting on a play describing the highlights of their trip.

The Feast of Thanksgiving did not originate with the Pilgrims. The current festivity did start with the pilgrims, and has become one of the defining and endearing practices of American culture. A similar event took place in Mexico. They did not adopt it as part of their national consciousness as we Americans have here in the USA.

I love our Thanksgiving holiday. For us, Hispanics, it is the beginning of our American

Southwest. All of the above named contributions and because it is the beginning of Catholic Christianity in the USA; before the pilgrims arrived in Massachusetts. The Story goes as follows:

In 1598, a gentlemen from Zacatecas, Don Juan de Oñate, a wealthy silver mine owner set out to explore north of the colonies. He united about 400 people for his caravan, 700 heads of cattle, including horses, cows, sheep and goats. Franciscan priests also were part of the group and upon arrival they celebrated with a high Mass thanking Divine Providence for surviving the terrible experience. It was not a dinner commemorating an event and thanking God for surviving a year in the new land but an immediate jest of gratitude to the creator for having passed through a most desolate desert and survived.

There is no comparison between the two events, but one is well known and the other one rarely, if ever, appears in the history books of this country.

We in this area continue to tell the story of our ancestors and celebrate the unification of cultures. Hispanics, being a product of both Native Americans and Europeans we hate to give precedence to one of the other, we love both. But of course the debate rages on, and many are angry we even talk about our Spanish heritage for the abuses the Spaniards committed upon the natives. On the other hand, the English are respected historically and we as Hispanics have much to learn about forgiving past deeds.

Our El Paso has made national history many

times in areas that surprise even us for example. Back

in 1957, we elected the first Mexican American mayor

of a major US City: Raymond I. Telles. One may think that it was San Antonio when they elected Henry Cisneros in the 70's or Federico Peña in Denver, Colorado but no it was Telles who also later became an Ambassador to the Central American Country of Costa Rica. Of course, prior to this land being the USA there were many Hispanic legislators, mayors and governors in the area all throughout California, Colorado, Arizona, New Mexico and Texas.

With Texas having a history of racism, it was El Paso back in 1962, 6 years before the 1968 Civil Rights legislation, that we passed a law desegregating public places. This was not spear headed by a Hispanic but a white man who had the courage to stand up for what he knew was wrong. His name was Bert Williams, and he later became Mayor of the City.

We also made history when in the 60's Texas Western College Coach Dan Haskins put together an all black lineup for his basketball team and we became national champions.

And it was in Texas, thanks to a Black El Paso Doctor named Lawrence Nixon, that Blacks were given the right to vote in all of Texas and this case went all the way to the US Supreme Court. The year was 1924.

Being close to El Paso gave Mexico an opportunity to oust the monarchy imposed by Napoleon III as President Benito Juarez sheltered himself in our sister city who changed its name to Ciudad Juarez commemorating this event. They were afraid to attack him fearing a reprisal from the USA. Eventually they retreated and Benito Juarez was able to resume his presidency.

So year after year, there have been reasons to thank God for being a border city where progressive thinking sometimes came before the rest of the nation.

This is an area where Black, Anglos, Mexicans and natives have lived in peace, not always harmoniously, but in civility. To date, we are one of the safest cities in the nation in spite of living next door to one of the most violent cities of the 21st century, Ciudad Juarez.

Another success in this city has been the peaceful co-existence of Arabs and Jews. While they may fight in other cities, here they are harmonious and share even shopping establishments who cater to Middle Easter foods. One of our most beloved artists in the area boasts and rejoices in his Arabic-Jewish roots, Hal Marcus. He is a painter and a Musician.

CHAPTER SEVEN

"A two-nation city with three adjacent States"

There is an area in the USA called Four Corners, where four states mingle: California, Colorado, Utah and New Mexico. Here in El Paso, we are sandwiched between New Mexico, USA and Old Mexico. This little protrusion of Texas is unique because it shares most of its history with New Mexico and Mexico but politically it is part of the State of Texas. Our Mexican counterpart is the State of Chihuahua.

Most of the inhabitants of the area have ties in both countries Mexico and the US, not so much nowadays but the cultural ties are still strong. It is not uncommon to hear a monolingual person complain about why people prefer to speak Spanish. However more than 80% of the population speak both languages.

Being a military town, this is still a problem but I would say that we are getting better. However, the younger generations either reject knowing Spanish or embrace it totally once they leave the area and realize the uniqueness and advantages of having this bicultural, bilingual heritage. I think the more educated the populace becomes, the more they realize that being bilingual and bicultural is a great asset.

As I am writing this, I am very hopeful that we are being more aware of who we are as a people and of our contributions. No need to prove who is better but that we are part of a whole and just as important as anybody else.

White Texas was part of Spain, they left us with an enormous legacy of schools, ranches, wineries, hospitals, churches, libraries. They taught us about art, music, dance, medicine, ranching, theater and religion. From the natives we learned how to live in the desert, use local plants as medicine and respect the environment. Natives thank the animals for their contributions and thank them for permitting them to eat their meat.

When the Anglos joined our communities, we learned about the beliefs of the founding fathers, how to form non-profits, how to create clubs, voluntary firemen, election of the people.

As we became part of a huge country that accepted immigrants from all over the world, we started seeing a more varied population. When World

War II happened, we saw the population of Germans and Italians grown in our city.

We also saw the population of Arabs from Lebanon, Syria and Palestine, as well as an influx of Jews and Mormons. So our city became multinational in many ways. The beauty of this is that people of different religions, spoke different languages, ate different foods yet they got along. Different parts of the city housed many immigrants from China, Japan, Germany and Poland. El Paso is not only Anglo, Native and Hispanic but has become an International city.

CHAPTER EIGHT

"Personal accomplishments"

Having the entrepreneurial spirit of my mom, I have embarked on many endeavors trying to find a niche where I could excel. When I was going to college, I had three jobs. I managed the night desk of a local business school every evening, I did the bookkeeping for a local art gallery and I did the billing for a furniture store.

Only in my last semester of college, I went to school for a whole semester and enjoyed it, dedicating myself to the study of business management. My first job was with a mortgage company as soon as I got my BBA from our University of Texas back in 1975. I really loved the idea of helping people achieve their goal of acquiring a home so I ventured to learn all I could on how to apply for a loan, how to get one, and how to get good credit and pay off a home as soon as possible.

I worked for various mortgage companies in various capacities and even was offered to acquire the branch of a Mortgage Company. I let the opportunity go when I decided to get married and ended up going to Europe and Africa as a housewife. It would have been a wonderful accomplishment, but I chose to be a wife instead. I ended up regretting that decision, but I would not have acquired the understanding of being an American and having self worth had I not been in a failed marriage away from the US. I learned to appreciate the freedoms that nowadays are taken for granted.

When I got back from Africa, I worked many years as a mortgage banker and eventually started a lingerie shop. I always wanted to have a store. Someone offered to send me lingerie from France so I took the opportunity and started a boutique. I worked on this endeavor for two years.

The supply chain was not consistent and I had to shut down. In the meantime, I learned a lot about importing and retail stores. In order to keep it going, I worked over 12 hours a day, seven days a week. Later on I ended up going out of town to San Antonio to work with some friends that were starting a mortgage company. I loved my worked but the Tejano culture was not my cup of tea, so I decided to come back to El Paso.

I transitioned from Mortgage banking to credit counseling, which really enriched my soul helping families attain their goals. I had a wonderful idea to start a Housing Fair to unite Mortgage companies, banks, builders, title companies, credit consultants, realtors and have an event where the local community would benefit by getting the information all in one place.

I ended up forming a great coalition and more than 5,000 people attended. The ugly face of politics entered, however, and the Democrats could nor believe a Republican had accomplished this. They decided to oust me from my creation. I was so disillusioned that I started looking for something else to do.

I belonged to an organization that hosted international visitors from all over the world to our city and had even ended up being president of the organization. Representing it various years in Washington, I was eventually recruited to work with that program in Washington, Frankly, I was scared to death having to work 24/7 but I love traveling and this would give me the opportunity to know my country better but being away from friends and family was scary.

Nevertheless, I applied and within three months ended up in Washington DC with my first assignment, to host financial bankers and managers from 26 different countries for almost a month crisscrossing the USA. This job required me to know how the government works, US Geography and

History plus knowledge of the arts. I love museums, art galleries, theater, opera, ballet, sports, universities and learning from people so I was doing all that I like, plus all events paid by the Government. For almost 20 years, I was in heaven and travelled throughout the country. I was able to visit 48 of our 50 states. I am only missing Maine and Hawaii.

During this period I made friends from all over the world and was invited to visit many of their countries which I did at every opportunity or free time I had. My knowledge of the world quadrupled, I learned to love and respect people from all over the world. I loved the fact that I stopped judging and learned to respect and honor people from all walks of life, religions, races, cultures. Being different to me meant that I could learn from someone totally different from me. I loved the time I spent as a Cultural interpreter for the US Department of State. I loved showing off my country and learning every day some new aspect of my beautiful USA.

Another plus was being introduced to the different immigrants that live in the USA and how they form communities to preserve their various cultural differences and how they can contribute to the enhancement of our society. When I would encounter a toxic person, I had to remember that they were our guests and despite their ill behavior my job was to respect them and try to learn from them as well as try that that person understood why we behave the way we do, It was a trying endeavor but if successful we could build bridges with people that could become our enemies.

CHAPTER NINE

"How to welcome an unexpected birth"

One of the most interesting occurrences I lived was helping an international visitor that came being very pregnant. After the long plain ride from Africa, she came in and within a couple of hours the premature birth of her child was triggered. I had no idea what to do, how to behave and how to take care of a visitor giving birth, but what started being a nightmare ended up being a cathartic experience for me and opportunity for growth.

During my marriage I traveled to Europe and Africa when I was 7 months pregnant. I wanted my baby to meet his father because I grew up without one and I did not want my child to have that experience. Everyone I knew suggested I have my baby here in US, but I did not listen because I wanted my baby to be born in the mist of the love between his two parents.

I had started taking the pill before we got married to make sure that I would not get pregnant until my husband was through with his obliged service with the Algerian army for two years, and then we would have our child either here in US or in Algeria. God, however, had another plan.

Despite our provisions to not get pregnant, I ended up pregnant within a month after we were married. We were happy, and once he was settled in Algeria, I went to France to buy a car to take to Algeria and we proceeded to Africa. It was a wonderful experience because we brought my husband's father from Paris to Algeria after he had a minor surgery.

It was wonderful to have a father because to me, he became my father after I was married to his eldest son. I never had a father. I met my dad the day I got married and never knew what having a father was like. It turns out that my father in law had lived with Spaniards that were living in Algeria prior to the independence of Algeria from France so he and his wife had the opportunity to learn Spanish through the several years they lived in a condominium where several Spaniard families lived.

He had not spoken Spanish for at least a decade and meeting me was refreshing since he did not know English and I did not know Arabic, but he knew Spanish and we got along beautifully. Sidi was a gentle soul, loved his eldest son and accepted me as his daughter from the moment I met him, so I gained a father during my stay in Algeria.

However, something happened and in my eighth month after a very healthy pregnancy period, my water burst and I gave birth. The medical staff kept referring to my baby as a fetus. To me it was a child. I gave birth all by myself since the nurses refused to help me since I was an American. An Algerian woman that had a bed by mine came to my assistance and helped me give birth. The Doctor got there after the baby was already being held by me. As soon as they came, she was taken from me and I did not see her until hours later when my husband arrived and they took us to the incubator where she was.

I was in shock. They did not let me hold her and there was a cockroach inside the incubator. I could not even talk. I was totally helpless. My husband was furious about the conditions, and he and the staff got into a big argument. Hours later, my baby was dead. They never let us see her and she was taken to a common grave, with no personal services. I was devastated, angry, and sad beyond comprehension. I became a moving corpse, as well. This was the end of our relationship since I asked him after the experience to please let me come back to the USA. I did not want to be in Algeria one additional moment.

I developed a dislike for fanatic Muslims that hated Americans, whether they knew us or not. Just being American was enough for you to become the target for their hatred. I just wanted to stay away from them.

So, these type of feelings were definitely not who I was. I am incapable of hatred but I was hurt and did not even want to be close to anything Arab or Muslim.

I found myself working with many Arabs, despite this. I was beginning to feel uneasy and unhappy. I was assigned to work with a huge group of international visitors. I went with the group to the first tour of DC to show them the beautiful city. When I got back and was ready to go to bed, I got called to attend the final visitor that finally showed up. So, I got dressed and headed to find my visitor. Upon arrival to her room, I find a beautiful black lady dressed with an attire trying to conceal a huge belly. I greeted her and asked her if the State Department knew she was pregnant. She said "No. I tried to conceal my pregnancy because I wanted to come, and if they knew I was pregnant they would have taken me out of the program." I said "Ok, now you had a very heavy voyage, how do you feel?" She said "I feel fine but I am tired."

I had her review her itinerary and sign all the welcoming documents. Then I asked her to call me in the morning when she was ready so I could take her to have breakfast with the group and introduce her. She was a beautiful women, highly educated and with an elegant demeaner I called the person in charge of the program and prepared her to possible conflict.

What happened next was both beautiful and troubling. Pregnant women in advanced, stages of pregnancy, were not encouraged to participate in these programs because our itineraries were hectic and very strenuous for a pregnant woman. We had to always be prepared for any contingencies.

It was obvious to me that she new this, and that she had done everything to conceal the pregnancy because she wanted her child to be born here in the USA.

When we took her to the hospital, the State Department contacted her embassy and they were supposed to be in charge of her citizen. I was told to leave her in the hospital, make sure that she was fully attended and then I could leave. I was prepared to do this but the baby came in quickly and she started having strong contractions so I decided to stay with her in the hospital until her baby was born.

I had never encountered such a situation before, other than about 20 years before I had been pregnant by myself in a foreign country and knew first-hand how helpless one feels. I stayed with her, held her hand and was by her side until the baby was born and was fully attended to. It was a beautiful birth, but she was very scared and almost broke my hand trying to get rid of her pain. I had to be by her side, reassure her and give her tender loving care like I would have wanted I to have when I was in Algeria.

I learned a few things during this ordeal. For one, I did not know that black babies are born white and as their bodies adjust to the environment they start getting darker pigmentation. The hospital we were in was state of the art. The rooms were like hotel bedrooms and quite cozy and beautiful. This woman I was helping had mirrors where she could see all that was happening. Next to her bed, a beautiful crib with warming lights and about 4 doctors awaited the infant. They put soft music and it was the most beautiful birth I had ever seen in a movie or the one I experienced.

Imagine… I had been treated by African Muslims with the most disdain and antagonistic behavior. I made my mind that I would never ever treat someone like they had treated me. I had to be better and show how our society treats foreigners. I treated her as if she was my daughter and the infant was my grandchild. This experience healed my heart and replaced the memory of the birth I had experienced by one full of love and respect.

Many of us in the group went to visit her afterward, bought her clothes and whatever she needed while her embassy made preparations to take her back to Africa. While we were in DC we kept visiting her in the hospital and wished her well.

CHAPTER TEN

"An encounter with a figment of my imagination

An unexpected happening."

I love going to Museums, especially the Metropolitan Museum in New York. I always made it a point to take my International visitors to the best museums in the country, especially on certain evenings when the museums open at night. I would always go to see the new exhibits with the visitors of by myself.

One day I was in New York and went by myself to see an exhibit of Roman faces painted on Egyptian sarcophagus. It was one of the most beautiful exhibits I had ever seen. I spent hours admiring these beautiful Roman faces in colorful sarcophagus. I was particularly attracted to one that had an extremely beautiful Roman young man. By chance, they had a picture of it in the Museum store and I went ahead and purchased the photo. I took it home and placed it in a frame by my bed. This man was so handsome plus his face exuded peace and beauty. I nicknamed "ROMANITO" meaning little Roman. Since I was by myself I started talking to him and telling him how my day went and be became like my best friend.

A year or two passed by and on one of my assignments as I was greeting my International visitors one night, a visitor showed up who looked exactly like the Roman in the Museum. Now this was not a young man, but a man with exactly the same facial features as the Roman in my photo, even his hair was curly and black. When he introduced himself

I felt like my Romanito had come to life. It was the most fascinating experience that I have ever had.

I was smitten by this person that looked so much like my photo friend. I guess things happen for a reason. This person and I became very good friends throughout his stay in the USA. It was like I had known him all my life. I even went to visit him in his country and met his friends and family. It has been over 25 years since this happened and to date, we are still good friends.

You never know when you will meet a person that will be important to you all your life.

CHAPTER ELEVEN

Before I conclude this memoir, I want to share two incidents that happened to me that enabled me to remember my mom's wise words. She always told me that no matter what I was doing, God was able to see my behavior. If I was not acknowledged, that was not the purpose of the experience, but the manner in which I approached the challenge.

So with these thoughts in mind, on my last year of college, I had several jobs. One of them was working for an export firm that produced its merchandise in Mexico and was distributing in the US. It was my job to bill the recipients of our furniture and make sure that they paid. It was a very rewarding experience and I loved my job.

Several ladies before me had left this job, and I soon realized why. I was a young girl in my late teens, and I evidently had sparked attention from the manager, who also happened to be a small part owner of the firm. It seemed that every time I encountered him, he found a way to rub his body against mine.

At the beginning, I thought he just unknowingly rubbed against me and apologized, but it kept happening and I started being perturbed by this behavior. One time It really upset me and I asked him to please stop this behavior. He just laughed and started chasing me around the office. I immediately left and contacted my supervisor. She was devastated and said we should call the previous ladies that held that job. We did, and to our surprise, they all had similar experiences. I decided to contact the owner and tell him what was going on.

We documented the event and got written statements by some of the ladies involved and presented it to our boss. To my surprise, the owner told me that he had documented who I was and realized that I was the granddaughter of a girlfriend he had in his youth. They used to dance for a theater troupe and he had the most pleasant memories of my grandmother.

He was glad that he was in a position to right a wrong and hoped that I would not leave the company. The man harassing me was ultimately fired, even though he was part owner. I was very fortunate to find a man of values protecting me (the owner.) Plus, I found the courage to speak out and not let anyone disrespect me. I needed the job but I was not going to permit abuse from anyone based on financial need So thanks to my mother, I had the right attitude.

Another incident happened to me many years later while I was working for an International company as a Supervisor. I had been appointed by the President of the company to be the liaison between the factory workers and management.

One day the ladies that had to take or retrieve merchandise to their departments. Once the merchandise arrived, they approached me and said that they were very uncomfortable in the shipping area because some of the workers had pictures of naked women in the work area and they felt disrespected, but the men refused to take them down. I then went to the area and discovered that they were indeed having to walk around an area where pictures of exposed working women were hanging. I myself felt that it was not respectful to the women that worked in the area. I told the young men to please take those pictures down and they refused, they laughed and felt I was being unreasonable.

No matter how I felt, I went to talk to the main supervisors of the area. They were laughing at my request. I was upset, but decided to try another approach. I went to the nearest magazine supplier and bought several magazines that had naked men. I took them to my office and placed them in frames and put them in the walls of my office. By the way, top management went to my office often and not long after, the President of the company came to my office to talk to me.

I shared calmly what had transpired and told him that if management saw no wrong in letting employees have naked women in public areas then I had no reason to believe that it was wrong for me to admire naked men in my office. He laughed and said: "you fought this with intelligence. I will make sure that all those photos will be thrown in the garbage and the women as well as the men are respected in the work place." So, deed accomplished! I learned that if you get upset and retaliate you get nowhere. You need to think wisely and be devoid of anger.

My mom worked for 18 years in Mexico while she was a very young and inexperienced young lady but was trained by one of my uncles who taught her to approach problems with a calm attitude and always behave like a lady and demand respect from co-workers. I was very fortunate to have such guidance in my life. I definitely learned that anytime I let anger take over, the outcome was never successful.

EPILOGUE

I hope you enjoyed my memories! I have many, but these are the ones that have impacted my life most of all.

What I have learned is that life is a magnificent journey with ups and downs. Every person has a different path and a different mission.

We, in the US, have been very blessed to live in a country where we still have the freedom to know, meet, and enjoy the company of people from all over the world and we are free to express our likes and dislikes. We are free to ask, as long as we are respectful and learn from everyone. We just have to be open and loving to each person and treat them like we like to be treated.

Living in a country that values freedom is very important. I had the choice of picking a career that I wanted. Marrying a person that was totally different from me, opening various businesses which at the time I thought is what I wanted to do and shut them down if it was not what I wanted. Living in the cities of my choice, having friends from all walks of life.

When I was in college, I wanted to be an interpreter with the UN. Chose to be a mortgage banker, much later I did become an interpreter with the US DEPT of State. I opened my first business as a mortgage banker, I became a Credit Counselor, A Real Estate Agent. An Appraiser, A started a Lingerie Shop, I got a certification to be a Reiki Master and my greatest accomplishment was importing Olive Oil from Greece, that was a wonderful adventure. I knew nothing about these enterprises but I tried it.

I also was able to build the house I wanted and furnish it just the way I wanted, travel the world and live an independent life. I don't know where my next step with be but I am glad I am alive and that I still have the will of life and enjoy life.

Later in life, I chose to leave everything and be the caretaker of my mother, the woman that did everything in her power and throughout her life to make me a good accomplished human being, It was hard to take care of someone 24/7 but sometimes one has to sacrifice for others. The Bible says that we will be blessed if we take care of our parents so I am waiting for my blessing. Life is a blessing, and to date, I am healthy even at my age.

Que viva la vida! Blessings from the Diamond in the Desert.

ABOUT THE AUTHOR

Ms. Vasquez is dedicated to Women trying to find a purpose in life. She wants to leave a legacy to other women so that they can benefit from her struggles. She is dedicated to her Country, her family and those who made it a challenge, as well as the many strangers who wonder how life is in the USA for multi-cultural families.

Ms. Vasquez believes Life is a gift. Many times, she has wondered if she had a purpose. After she retired and remembered events or encounters throughout her lifetime, she realized she had been touched by and had touched many lives with positive outcomes.

These are her memories that she has shared with you. She hopes you realize that life is a wonderful challenge, worthy of being emulated or used as an example of what not to do. She wants you to enjoy her story, learn from her mistakes and see her victories as lessons.

Concepción Carolina Vásquez is the only daughter of a valiant woman from an area of the US that borders with Mexico. She likes to think of herself as binational.

She emerged from a fusion of immigrants of Mexico, Spain, Scandinavia and natives from the present USA. Her religion is Catholic and God has always played a very important role in her life.

Ms. Vasquez grew up loving both countries: The USA, where she was born, and Mexico, where she grew up. She was taught from childhood to love the USA, honor its values, be a productive member of the community and always be proud and honored about her heritage. She was taught the history of both countries and both languages, as well as the customs of each. She was taught to never put one above the other, and to always be an American.